55th Annual Meeting of the Association for Computational Linguistics (ACL 2017)

Tutorial Abstracts

Vancouver, Canada
30 July – 4 August 2017

ISBN: 978-1-5108-4571-8

Printed from e-media with permission by:

Curran Associates, Inc.
57 Morehouse Lane
Red Hook, NY 12571

Some format issues inherent in the e-media version may also appear in this print version.

Printed by Curran Associates, Inc. (2017)

Association for Computational Linguistics
209 N. Eighth Street
Stroudsburg, Pennsylvania 18360

Phone: 1-570-476-8006
Fax: 1-570-476-0860

acl@aclweb.org

Additional copies of this publication are available from:

Curran Associates, Inc.
57 Morehouse Lane
Red Hook, NY 12571 USA
Phone: 845-758-0400
Fax: 845-758-2633
Email: curran@proceedings.com
Web: www.proceedings.com

ACL 2017

The 55th Annual Meeting of the Association for Computational Linguistics

Proceedings of the Conference Tutorial Abstracts

July 30 - August 4, 2017
Vancouver, Canada

Introduction

This volume contains the abstracts of the ACL 2017 tutorials. This year we had a joint call-for-tutorials, coordinated with the EACL and EMNLP co-chairs (6 co-chairs in total). We received 26 submissions for the joint ACL/EACL/EMNLP call, and it was a difficult task to make a final selection. The six co-chairs applied the following criteria for evaluation: relevance to ACL community, quality of proposal, quality of instructor, estimate of attendance, relevance of area. The tutorials were then assigned to venues trying to respect proposers' preferences and to balance topics across venues. Nine tutorials had ACL as the preferred conference, from which one was rejected, two were redirected to EMNLP and the rest (six of them) was accepted. All six are organised as half-day tutorials.

We are very grateful to Alex Klementiev and Lucia Specia (EACL tutorial chairs), Nathan Schneider and Alexandra Birch (EMNLP tutorial chairs), Priscilla Rasmussen and Anoop Sarkar (local chairs), Wei Lu, Sameer Singh and Margaret Mitchell (publication chairs), Min-Yen Kan and Regina Barzilay (program co-chairs) and of course Chris Callison-Burch (general chair) for various kinds of help, advice and assistance offered during the process of putting the tutorial programme and materials together. Most importantly, we would like to thank the tutorial presenters for the time and effort in preparing and presenting the tutorials.

We hope you will enjoy the tutorials!

ACL 2017 Tutorial Chairs
Maja Popović, Humboldt-Universität zu Berlin
Jordan Boyd-Graber, University of Colorado, Boulder

Tutorial Chairs:

Maja Popović, Humboldt-Universität zu Berlin
Jordan Boyd-Graber, University of Colorado, Boulder

Table of Contents

Conference Program

Sunday, July 30th

Morning Session

9:00–12:30 *NLP for Precision Medicine*
Hoifung Poon, Chris Quirk, Kristina Toutanova and Wen-tau Yih

9:00–12:30 *Multimodal Machine Learning: Integrating Language, Vision and Speech*
Louis-Philippe Morency and Tadas Baltrušaitis

9:00–12:30 *Deep Learning for Semantic Composition*
Xiaodan Zhu and Edward Grefenstette

Afternoon Session

14:00–17:30 *Deep Learning for Dialogue Systems*
Yun-Nung Chen, Asli Celikyilmaz and Dilek Hakkani-Tür

14:00–17:30 *Beyond Words: Deep Learning for Multiword Expressions and Collocations*
Valia Kordoni

14:00–17:30 *Tutorial: Making Better Use of the Crowd*
Jennifer Wortman Vaughan

NLP for Precision Medicine

Hoifung Poon[1] **Chris Quirk**[1] **Kristina Toutanova**[2] **Wen-tau Yih**[1]
[1] Microsoft Research, Redmond, WA, USA
[2] Google Research, Seattle, WA, USA
{hoifung,chrisq,scottyih}@microsoft.com
kristout@google.com

1 Tutorial Overview

We will introduce precision medicine and showcase the vast opportunities for NLP in this burgeoning field with great societal impact. We will review pressing NLP problems, state-of-the art methods, and important applications, as well as datasets, medical resources, and practical issues. The tutorial will provide an accessible overview of biomedicine, and does not presume knowledge in biology or healthcare. The ultimate goal is to reduce the entry barrier for NLP researchers to contribute to this exciting domain. Our motivation stems from the shocking inefficiency of medicine today. For the top 20 prescription drugs in the US, 80% of patients are non-responders. The result is ineffective care delivery, which leads to missed opportunities for treatment and constitutes a large part of the estimated trillion-billion waste in the US health system each year. Recent technological disruptions such as $1000 human genome have enabled more personalized and effective treatments, with great potential to improve patient health and save lives.

A major bottleneck to advancing precision medicine is access to structured information encoded in free text. In cancer, for example, it takes hours for a molecular tumor board of many specialists to review one patient's genomics data and make treatment decisions. With 1.7 million new cancer patients in the US alone each year, this is clearly not scalable. Most relevant knowledge resides in published literature, whereas rich patient information is scattered in clinical notes in electronic medical records (EMRs). NLP holds the key to unlock such structured information for supporting predictive analytics and medical decision making. Compared to the newswire and web domains, healthcare also exhibits important differences and offers a fertile ground of novel research challenges.

In this tutorial, we will first present an overview of precision medicine, and highlight key research challenges and opportunities for NLP. We will then dive into main research areas and review problem formulations and cutting-edge methods. To illustrate the potential impact of NLP, we will present several real-world applications with promising results. To facilitate new entry to the filed, we will provide a systematic review of relevant resources and conclude with a list of exciting open problems.

2 Outline

1. Precision Medicine (20 minutes)
   - Motivation: imprecise medicine, disruptions, what successes look like
   - Challenges: knowledge, reasoning
   - Opportunities for NLP
2. Annotation Bottleneck (25 minutes)
   - Example tasks: entity linking, relation extraction
   - Distant supervision
   - Learning with indirect supervision
3. Extract complex structured information (25 minutes)
   - Example task: complex event extraction
   - Grounded semantic parsing
4. Beyond the sentence boundary (25 minutes)
   - Motivation: knowledge extraction for molecular tumor board
   - Cross-sentence relation extraction
   - Graph LSTM
5. Reasoning (25 minutes)
   - Standard approaches and challenges

Proceedings of the 55th Annual Meeting of the Association for Computational Linguistics-Tutorial Abstracts, pages 1–2
Vancouver, Canada, July 30 - August 4, 2017.
https://doi.org/10.18653/v1/P17-5001

- Neural embeddings of structured knowledge
- Example application: Knowledge base completion

6. Applications in Precision Medicine (30 minutes)
   - Decision support for molecular tumor board
   - Rational design of cancer drug combinations
   - Clinical machine reading
7. Resources (20 minutes)
   - Text, ontologies, and knowledge bases
   - Shared tasks
   - Practical issues: publishers, privacy, regulations
8. Open Problems (10 minutes)

3 Instructors

Hoifung Poon is a Researcher at Microsoft Research Redmond. His research interests lie in advancing machine learning and natural language processing (NLP) to help automate discovery and decision support in precision medicine. He received his Ph.D. in computer science & engineering at the University of Washington. His past work has been recognized with Best Paper Awards from premier NLP and machine learning venues such as NAACL-09 (unsupervised morphological segmentation), EMNLP-09 (unsupervised semantic parsing), and UAI-11 (sum-product networks).

Chris Quirk is a Principal Researcher at Microsoft Research Redmond. Since joining Microsoft Research in 2001, his research has focused on effective computational systems for aiding human communication, understanding, and task completion. His primary focus is in machine translation, building practical and widely-used system implementations and authoring a number of influential papers. He has also worked in paraphrase, information extraction, and most recently biological applications of natural language processing and machine learning. He has served on numerous program committees, acted Area Chair (ACL 2010, EMNLP 2012), and is currently an action editor of the TACL journal.

Kristina Toutanova is a Staff Research Scientist at Google Research Seattle and affiliate faculty member at the University of Washington. In 2005, she obtained her Ph.D. from the Computer Science Department at Stanford University, where she was advised by Christopher Manning. She focuses on modeling the structure of natural language using machine learning, in the areas of semantic parsing, knowledge extraction, information retrieval, and text-to-text generation. She has co-authored more than 50 publications at refereed conferences and journals, including four papers that have won awards at conferences (EMNLP, NAACL, CoNLL, ECML). She served as a program co-chair for CoNLL 2008 and ACL 2014 and is currently serving as a co-editor-in-chief of the TACL journal.

Wen-tau Yih is a Senior Researcher at Microsoft Research Redmond. His research interests include natural language processing, machine learning and information retrieval. Yih received his Ph.D. in computer science at the University of Illinois at Urbana-Champaign. His work on joint inference using integer linear programming (ILP) helped the UIUC team win the CoNLL-05 shared task on semantic role labeling, and the approach has been widely adopted in the NLP community since then. After joining MSR in 2005, he has worked on email spam filtering, keyword extraction and search & ad relevance. His recent work focuses on continuous semantic representations using neural networks and matrix/tensor decomposition methods, with applications in lexical semantics, knowledge base embedding and question answering. Yih received the best paper award from CoNLL-2011, an outstanding paper award from ACL-2015 and has served as area chairs (HLT-NAACL-12, ACL-14, EMNLP-16,17), program co-chairs (CEAS-09, CoNLL-14) and action/associated editors (TACL, JAIR) in recent years.

Multimodal Machine Learning: Integrating Language, Vision and Speech

Louis-Philippe Morency
Language Technologies Institute
Carnegie Mellon University
morency@cs.cmu.edu

Tadas Baltrušaitis
Language Technologies Institute
Carnegie Mellon University
tbaltrus@cs.cmu.edu

Abstract

Multimodal machine learning is a vibrant multi-disciplinary research field which addresses some of the original goals of artificial intelligence by integrating and modeling multiple communicative modalities, including linguistic, acoustic and visual messages. With the initial research on audio-visual speech recognition and more recently with language & vision projects such as image and video captioning and visual question answering, this research field brings some unique challenges for multimodal researchers given the heterogeneity of the data and the contingency often found between modalities.

Tutorial overview

The present tutorial will review fundamental concepts of machine learning and deep neural networks before describing the five main challenges in multimodal machine learning:

1. **Representation**: A first fundamental challenge is to learn how to represent and summarize the multimodal data to highlight the complementarity and synchrony between modalities. The heterogeneity of multimodal data makes it particularly challenging for coordinated and joint representations. For example, language is often seen as symbolic while audio and visual modalities will be represented as signals.

2. **Translation**: A second challenge is how to translate data from one modality to another. Not only is the data heterogeneous, but the relationship between modalities is often open-ended or subjective. For example, when describing a specific image verbally, more than one description can be correct. The evaluation and characterization of the multimodal translation may be subjective.

3. **Alignment**: A third challenge is to identify the direct relations between elements from two or more different modalities. For example, when analyzing the speech and gestures of a human subject, how can we align specific gestures with the spoken words or utterances? This alignment between modalities may be based on long-range dependencies and the segmentation is often ambiguous (e.g., words or utterances).

4. **Fusion**: A fourth challenge is to join information from two or more modalities to perform a prediction, discrete or continuous. For example, for audio-visual speech recognition, the visual descriptoin of the lip motion is fused with the speech signal to predict spoken words. The information coming from different modalities may have varying predictive power and noise topology. With possibly missing data in at least one of the modalities. Multimodal fusion needs to handle such variations.

5. **Co-learning**: A fifth challenge is to transfer knowledge between modalities and their representations. Exemplified by algorithms of co-training, conceptual grounding and zero shot learning, how does knowledge learning from one modality (e.g., predicted labels or representation) can help a computational model trained on a different modality? This challenge is particularly relevant when one of the modalities has limited resources (e.g., annotated data).

The tutorial will also present state-of-the-art algorithms that were recently proposed to solve mul-

Proceedings of the 55th Annual Meeting of the Association for Computational Linguistics-Tutorial Abstracts, pages 3–5
Vancouver, Canada, July 30 - August 4, 2017.
https://doi.org/10.18653/v1/P17-5002

timodal applications such as image captioning, video descriptions and visual question-answer. We will also discuss the current and upcoming challenges.

Structure

We plan to follow a similar structure to our ICMI 2016 tutorial which was 3 hours long:

1. Intruduction
   - What is Multimodal?
     - Historical view, multimodal vs multimedia
   - Why multimodal?
     - Multimodal applications: image captioning, video description, AVSR,
   - Core technical challenges
     - Representation learning, translation, alignment, fusion and co-learning
2. Basic concepts — Part 1
   - Linear models
     - Score and loss functions, regularization
   - Neural networks
     - Activation functions, multi-layer perceptron
   - Optimization
     - Stochastic gradient descent, backpropagation
3. Unimodal representations
   - Language representations
     - Distributional hypothesis and word embedding
   - Visual representations
     - Convolutional neural networks
   - Acoustic representations
     - Spectrograms, auto-encoders
4. Multimodal representations
   - Joint representations
     - Visual semantic spaces, multimodal auto-encoder
   - Coordinated representations
     - Component analysis
     - Similarity metrics, canonical correlation analysis

===Break===

1. Basic concepts — Part 2
   - Language models
     - Unigrams, bigrams, skip-grams, skip-thought
   - Unimodal sequence modeling
     - Recurrent neural networks, LSTMs
   - Optimization
     - Backpropagation through time
2. Multimodal translation and mapping
   - Encoder-decoder models
     - Machine translation, image captioning
   - Generative vs example based approaches
     - Viseme generation, visual puppetry
     - Model evaluation
3. Modality alignment
   - Latent alignment approaches
     - Attention models, multi instance learning
   - Explicit alignment
     - Dynamic time warping
4. Multimodal fusion and co-learning
   - Model free approaches
     - Early and late fusion, hybrid models
   - Kernel-based fusion
     - Multiple kernel learning
   - Multimodal graphical models
     - Factorial HMM, Multi-view Hidden CRF
   - Co-learning
     - Parallel, non-parallel and hybrid data
5. Future directions and concluding remarks

About the speakers

Louis-Philippe Morency (`https://www.cs.cmu.edu/~morency/`) is Assistant Professor in the Language Technology Institute at the Carnegie Mellon University where he leads the Multimodal Communication and Machine Learning Laboratory (MultiComp Lab). He received his Ph.D. and Master degrees from MIT Computer Science and Artificial Intelligence Laboratory. In 2008, Dr. Morency was selected as one of "AI's 10 to Watch" by IEEE Intelligent Systems. He has received 7 best paper awards in multiple ACM- and IEEE-sponsored conferences for his work on context-based gesture recognition, multimodal probabilistic fusion and computational models of human communication dynamics. Dr. Morency was General Chair for the International Conference on Multimodal Interaction (ICMI 2012) and the NIPS 2010 workshop on Modeling Human Communication Dynamics. He was Program Chair for ICMI 2011, 2014 and 2016, as well as the Tenth International Conference on Creating, Connecting and Collaborating through Computing in January 2012.

Tadas Baltrušaitis (`http://www.cl.cam.ac.uk/~tb346/`) is a post-doctoral associate at the Language Technologies Institute, Carnegie Mellon University. Before this, he was a post-doctoral research at the University of Cambridge, where he also received his PhD degree in 2014. His primary research interests lie in the automatic understanding of non-verbal human behaviour, computer vision, and multimodal machine learning. His papers have won a number of awards for his work on non-verbal human behavior analysis, including ICMI 2014 best student paper award, and ETRA 2016 emerging investigator award. He is also a winner of several challenges in computer vision and multi-modal machine learning, including FERA 2015, and AVEC 2011.

Deep Learning for Semantic Composition

Xiaodan Zhu
Queen's University
National Research Council Canada
zhu2048@gmail.com

Edward Grefenstette
DeepMind
etg@google.com

1 Tutorial Description

Learning representations to model the meaning of text has been a core problem in natural language understanding (NLP). The last several years have seen extensive interests on distributional approaches, in which text spans of different granularities are encoded as continuous vectors. If properly learned, such representations have been shown to help achieve the state-of-the-art performances on a variety of NLP problems.

In this tutorial, we will cover the fundamentals and selected research topics on neural network-based modeling for semantic composition, which aims to learn distributed representations for larger spans of text, e.g., phrases (Yin and Schütze, 2014) and sentences (Zhu et al., 2016; Chen et al., 2016; Zhu et al., 2015b,a; Tai et al., 2015; Kalchbrenner et al., 2014; Irsoy and Cardie, 2014; Socher et al., 2012), from the meaning representations of their parts, e.g., word embedding.

We begin by briefly introducing traditional approaches to semantic composition, including logic-based formal semantic approaches and simple arithmetic operations over vectors based on corpus word counts (Mitchell and Lapata, 2008; Landauer and Dumais, 1997).

Our main focus, however, will be on distributed representation-based modeling, whereby the representations of words and the operations composing them are jointly learned from a training objective. We cover the generic ideas behind neural network-based semantic composition and dive into the details of three typical composition architectures: the convolutional composition models (Kalchbrenner et al., 2014; Zhang et al., 2015), recurrent composition models (Zhu et al., 2016), and recursive composition models (Irsoy and Cardie, 2014; Socher et al., 2012; Zhu et al., 2015b; Tai et al., 2015). After that, we will discuss several unsupervised approaches (Le and Mikolov, 2014; Kiros et al., 2014; Bowman et al., 2016; Miao et al., 2016).

We will then advance to discuss several selected topics. We first cover the models that consider compositional with non-compositional (e.g., holistically learned) semantics (Zhu et al., 2016, 2015a). Next, we discuss composition models that integrate multiple architectures of neural networks. We also discuss semantic composition and decomposition (Turney, 2014). In the end we briefly discuss sub-word neural-network-based composition models (Zhang et al., 2015; Sennrich et al., 2016)

We will then summarize the tutorial, flesh out limitations of current approaches, and discuss future directions that are interesting to us.

2 Tutorial Outline

- Introduction
  - Definition of semantic composition
  - Conventional and basic approaches
    - Formal semantics
    - Bag of words with learned representations (additive, learned projection)
- Parametrising Composition Functions
  - Convolutional composition models
  - Recurrent composition models
  - Recursive composition models
    - TreeRNN/TreeLSTM
    - SPINN and RL-SPINN
  - Unsupervised models
    - Skip-thought vectors and paragraph vectors
    - Variational auto-encoders for text
- Selected Topics
  - Incorporating compositional and non-compositional (e.g., holistically learned) semantics
  - Integrating multiple composition architectures
  - Semantic composition and decomposition
  - Sub-word composition models
- Summary

Proceedings of the 55th Annual Meeting of the Association for Computational Linguistics-Tutorial Abstracts, pages 6–7
Vancouver, Canada, July 30 - August 4, 2017.
https://doi.org/10.18653/v1/P17-5003

3 Instructors

Xiaodan Zhu, Queen's University; National Research Council Canada.
zhu2048@gmail.com
`http://www.xiaodanzhu.com`
Xiaodan Zhu is an assistant professor of the Department of Electrical and Computer Engineering of Queen's University, Canada. Before that, he was a Research Officer of the National Research Council Canada. His research interests are in Natural Language Processing and Machine Learning. His recent work has focused on deep learning, semantic composition, sentiment analysis, and natural language inference.

Edward Grefenstette, Senior Research Scientist, DeepMind.
etg@google.com
`http://www.egrefen.com`
Edward Grefenstette is a Staff Research Scientist at DeepMind. His research covers the intersection of Machine Learning, Computer Reasoning, and Natural Language Understanding. Recent publications cover the topics of neural computation, representation learning at the sentence level, recognising textual entailment, and machine reading.

References

Samuel R. Bowman, Jon Gauthier, Abhinav Rastogi, Raghav Gupta, Christopher D. Manning, and Christopher Potts. 2016. A fast unified model for parsing and sentence understanding. In *ACL*.

Qian Chen, Xiaodan Zhu, Zhenhua Ling, Si Wei, and Hui Jiang. 2016. Enhancing and combining sequential and tree lstm for natural language inference. In *arXiv:1609.06038v1*.

Ozan Irsoy and Claire Cardie. 2014. Deep recursive neural networks for compositionality in language. In *NIPS*.

Nal Kalchbrenner, Edward Grefenstette, and Phil Blunsom. 2014. A convolutional neural network for modelling sentences. In *ACL*.

Ryan Kiros, Yukun Zhu, Ruslan Salakhutdinov, Richard Zemel, Antonio Torralba, Raquel Urtasun, and Sanja Fidler. 2014. Skip-thought vectors. In *arXiv:1506.06726*.

Thomas K Landauer and Susan T. Dumais. 1997. A solution to platos problem: The latent semantic analysis theory of acquisition, induction, and representation of knowledge. *Psychological Review* 104(2):211–240.

Quoc Le and Tomas Mikolov. 2014. Distributed representations of sentences and documents. In *ICML*.

Yishu Miao, Lei Yu, and Phil Blunsom. 2016. Neural variational inference for text processing. In *ICML*.

Jeff Mitchell and Mirella Lapata. 2008. Vector-based models of semantic composition. In *ACL*.

Rico Sennrich, Barry Haddow, and Alexandra Birch. 2016. Neural machine translation of rare words with subword units. In *ACL*.

Richard Socher, Brody Huval, Christopher D. Manning, and Andrew Y. Ng. 2012. Semantic compositionality through recursive matrix-vector spaces. In *EMNLP*.

Kai Sheng Tai, Richard Socher, and Christopher D. Manning. 2015. Improved Semantic Representations From Tree-Structured Long Short-Term Memory Networks. In *ACL*.

Peter Turney. 2014. Semantic composition and decomposition: From recognition to generation. In *arXiv:1405.7908*.

Wenpeng Yin and Hinrich Schütze. 2014. An exploration of embeddings for generalized phrases. In *ACL 2014 Student Research Workshop*.

Xiang Zhang, Junbo Zhao, and Yann LeCun. 2015. Character-level convolutional networks for text classification. In *NIPS*.

Xiaodan Zhu, Hongyu Guo, and Parinaz Sobhani. 2015a. Neural networks for integrating compositional and non-compositional sentiment in sentiment composition. In **SEM*.

Xiaodan Zhu, Parinaz Sobhani, and Hongyu Guo. 2015b. Long short-term memory over recursive structures. In *ICML*.

Xiaodan Zhu, Parinaz Sobhani, and Hongyu Guo. 2016. Dag-structured long short-term memory for semantic compositionality. In *NAACL*.

Deep Learning for Dialogue Systems

Yun-Nung Chen
National Taiwan University
Taipei, Taiwan
yvchen@ieee.org

Asli Celikyilmaz
Microsoft Research
Redmond, WA
asli@ieee.org

Dilek Hakkani-Tür
Google Research
Mountain View, CA
dilek@ieee.org

Abstract

In the past decade, goal-oriented spoken dialogue systems have been the most prominent component in today's virtual personal assistants. The classic dialogue systems have rather complex and/or modular pipelines. The advance of deep learning technologies has recently risen the applications of neural models to dialogue modeling. However, how to successfully apply deep learning based approaches to a dialogue system is still challenging. Hence, this tutorial is designed to focus on an overview of the dialogue system development while describing most recent research for building dialogue systems and summarizing the challenges, in order to allow researchers to study the potential improvements of the state-of-the-art dialogue systems. The tutorial material is available at http://deepdialogue.miulab.tw.

1 Tutorial Overview

With the rising trend of artificial intelligence, more and more devices have incorporated goal-oriented spoken dialogue systems. Among popular virtual personal assistants, Microsoft's Cortana, Apple's Siri, Amazon Alexa, Google Assistant, and Facebook's M, have incorporated dialogue system modules in various devices, which allow users to speak naturally in order to finish tasks more efficiently.

The traditional conversational systems have rather complex and/or modular pipelines. The advance of deep learning technologies has recently risen the applications of neural models to dialogue modeling. Nevertheless, applying deep learning technologies for building robust and scalable dialogue systems is still a challenging task and an open research area as it requires deeper understanding of the classic pipelines as well as detailed knowledge on the benchmark of the models of the prior work and the recent state-of-the-art work.

The goal of this tutorial is to provide the audience with developing trend of the dialogue systems, and a roadmap to get them started with the related work. In the first section of the tutorial, we motivate the work on conversation-based intelligent agents, in which the core underlying system is task-oriented dialogue systems. The second and third sections describe different approaches using deep learning for each component in the dialogue system and how it is evaluated. The last two sections focus on discussing the recent trends and current challenges on dialogue system technology and summarize the challenges and conclusions. Then the detailed content is described as follows.

2 Outline

1. Introduction & Background [15 min.]
    - Brief history of dialogue systems
    - Summarized challenges of intelligent assistants
    - Task-oriented dialogue system framework
    - Neural network basics
    - Reinforcement learning (RL) basics
2. Deep Learning Based Dialogue System [75 min.]
    - Spoken/Natural language understanding (SLU/NLU)
        - Semantic frame representation
        - Domain classification
        - Slot tagging
        - Joint semantic frame parsing
        - Contextual language understanding

Proceedings of the 55th Annual Meeting of the Association for Computational Linguistics-Tutorial Abstracts, pages 8–14
Vancouver, Canada, July 30 - August 4, 2017.
https://doi.org/10.18653/v1/P17-5004

- Structural language understanding
- Dialogue management (DM) – Dialogue state tracking (DST)
  - Neural belief tracker
  - Multichannel tracker
- Dialogue management (DM) – Policy optimization
  - Dialogue RL signal
  - Deep Q-network for learning policy
  - Hierarchical RL for learning policy
- Natural language generation (NLG)
  - Template-based NLG
  - Plan-based NLG
  - Class LM NLG
  - Phrase-based NLG
  - RNN-LM NLG
  - Semantic Conditioned LSTM
  - Structural NLG
  - Contextual NLG

3. Evaluation [10 min.]
   - Crowdsourcing
   - User simulation
4. Recent Trends on Learning Dialogues [45 min.]
   - End-to-end neural dialogue systems
     - Chit-chat seq2seq model
     - E2E joint NLU and DM
     - E2E supervised dialogue system
     - E2E memory network for dialogues
     - E2E RL-based *InfoBot*
     - E2E LSTM-based dialogue control
     - E2E RL-based task-completion bot
   - Dialogue breath
     - Domain adaptation
     - Intent expansion
     - Policy for domain adaptation
   - Dialogue depth
     - High-level intent for dialogue planning
     - Multimodality in dialogue systems
5. Challenges & Conclusions [5 mins]

3 Dialogue System Basics

This section will motivate the work on conversation-based intelligent agents, in which the core underlying system is task-oriented spoken dialogue systems.

The section starts with an overview of the standard pipeline framework for dialogue system illustrated in Figure 1 (Tur and De Mori, 2011). Basic components of a dialog system are automatic speech recognition (ASR), language understanding (LU), dialogue management (DM), and natural language generation (NLG) (Rudnicky et al., 1999; Zue et al., 2000; Zue and Glass, 2000).. This tutorial will mainly focus on LU, DM, and NLG parts.

Language Understanding Traditionally, domain identification and intent prediction are framed as utterance classification problems, where several classifiers such as support vector machines and maximum entropy have been employed (Haffner et al., 2003; Chelba et al., 2003; Chen et al., 2014). Then slot filling is framed as a word sequence tagging task, where the IOB (in-out-begin) format is applied for representing slot tags, and hidden Markov models (HMM) or conditional random fields (CRF) have been employed for slot tagging (Pieraccini et al., 1992; Wang et al., 2005; Raymond and Riccardi, 2007).

Dialogue Management A partially observable Markov decision process (POMDP) has been shown to be beneficial by allowing the dialogue manager to be optimized to plan and act under the uncertainty created by noisy speech recognition and semantic decoding (Williams and Young, 2007; Young et al., 2013). The POMDP policy controlling the actions taken by the system is trained in an episodic reinforcement learning (RL) framework whereby the agent receives a reinforcement signal after each dialogue (episode) reflecting how well it performed (Sutton and Barto, 1998). In addition, the dialogue states should be tracked in order to measure the belief of the current situation during the whole interaction (Young et al., 2010; Sun et al., 2014).

Natural Language Generation There are two NLG approaches, one focuses on generating text using templates or rules (linguistic) methods, the another uses corpus-based statistical techniques (Oh and Rudnicky, 2002). Oh and Rudnicky showed that stochastic generation benefits from two factors: 1) it takes advantage of the practical language of a domain expert instead of the developer and 2) it restates the problem in terms of classification and labeling, where expertise is not required for developing a rule-based generation system.

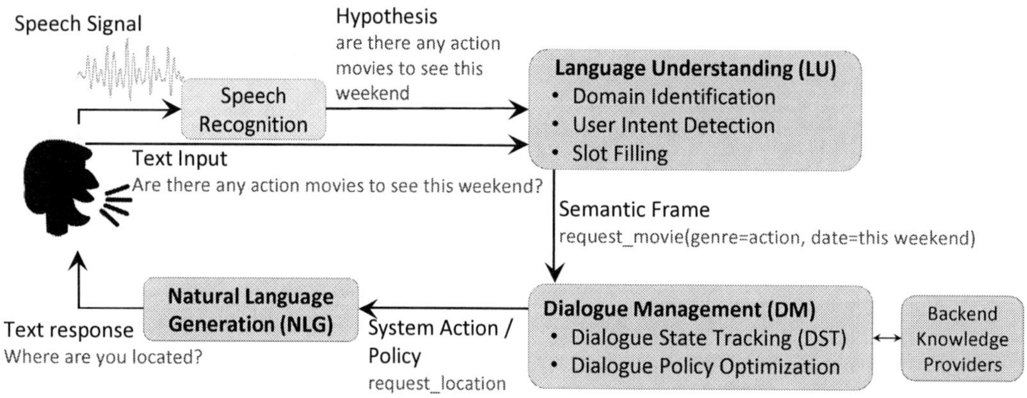

Figure 1: Pipeline framework of spoken dialog system.

W	find	action	movies	this	weekend
	↓	↓	↓	↓	↓
S	O	B-genre	O	B-date	I-date
I	find_movie				

Figure 2: An example utterance with annotations of semantic slots in IOB format (S) and intent (I), B-date and I-date denote the date slot.

4 Deep Learning Based Dialogue System

With the power of deep learning, there is increasing research work focusing on applying deep learning for each component.

Language Understanding With the advances on deep learning, deep belief networks (DBNs) with deep neural networks (DNNs) have been applied to domain and intent classification tasks (Sarikaya et al., 2011; Tur et al., 2012; Sarikaya et al., 2014). Recently, Ravuri and Stolcke (2015) proposed an RNN architecture for intent determination. For slot filling, deep learning has been viewed as a feature generator and the neural architecture can be merged with CRFs (Xu and Sarikaya, 2013). Yao et al. (2013) and Mesnil et al. (2015) later employed RNNs for sequence labeling in order to perform slot filling. Such architectures have later been extended to jointly model intent detection and slot filling in multiple domains (Hakkani-Tür et al., 2016; Jaech et al., 2016). End-to-end memory networks have been shown to provide a good mechanism for integrating longer term knowledge context and shorter term dialogue context into these models (Chen et al., 2016b,c). In addition, the importance of the LU module is investigated in Li et al. (2017a), where different types of errors from LU may degrade the whole system performance in an reinforcement learning setting.

Dialogue Management The state-of-the-art dialog managers focus on monitoring the dialog progress by neural dialog state tracking models. Among the initial models are the RNN based dialog state tracking approaches (Henderson et al., 2013) that has shown to outperform Bayesian networks (Thomson and Young, 2010). More recent work on Neural Dialog Managers that provide conjoint representations between the utterances, slot-value pairs as well as knowledge graph representations (Wen et al., 2016; Mrkšić et al., 2016) demonstrate that using neural dialog models can overcome current obstacles of deploying dialogue systems in larger dialog domains.

Natural Language Generation The RNN-based models have been applied to language generation for both chit-chat and task-orientated dialogue systems (Vinyals and Le, 2015; Wen et al., 2015b). The RNN-based NLG can learn from unaligned data by jointly optimizing sentence planning and surface realization, and language variation can be easily achieved by sampling from output candidates (Wen et al., 2015a). Moreover, Wen et al. (2015b) improved the prior work by adding a gating mechanism for controlling the dialogue act during generation in order to avoid semantics repetition, showing promising results.

5 Recent Trends and Challenges on Learning Dialogues

This part will focus on discussing the recent trends and current challenges on dialogue system technology.

End-to-End Learning for Dialogue System With the power of neural networks, there are more and more attempts for learning dialogue systems in an end-to-end fashion. Different learning frameworks are applied, including supervised learning and reinforcement learning. This part will discuss the work about end-to-end learning for dialogues (Dhingra et al., 2016; Wen et al., 2016; Williams and Zweig, 2016; Zhao and Eskenazi, 2016; Li et al., 2017b).

Recent advance of deep learning has inspired many applications of neural models to dialogue systems. Wen et al. (2016) and Bordes and Weston (2016) introduced a network-based end-to-end trainable task-oriented dialogue system, which treated dialogue system learning as the problem of learning a mapping from dialogue histories to system responses, and applied an encoder-decoder model to train the whole system. However, the system is trained in a supervised fashion, thus requires a lot of training data, and may not be able to explore the unknown space that does not exist in the training data for an optimal and robust policy.

Zhao and Eskenazi (2016) first presented an end-to-end reinforcement learning (RL) approach to dialogue state tracking and policy learning in the DM. This approach is shown to be promising when applied to a task-oriented system, which is to guess the famous person a user thinks of. In the conversation, the agent asks the user a series of Yes/No questions to find the correct answer. Dhingra et al. (2016) proposed an end-to-end differentiable KB-Infobot to improve the flexibility of question types and robustness. Li et al. (2017b) further presented an end-to-end neural dialogue system for completing tasks, which supported flexible question types, allowed user-initiated requests during conversation, and finally achieved better robustness.

Dialogue Breath In order to extend the coverage of the systems, transfer learning has been applied to different extended systems in order to proceed to a multi-domain scenario. Chen et al. (2016a) transfered the dialogue acts across different domains so that the performance of the newly-developed domain can be boosted. Kim et al. proposed to learn a domain-specific and domain-independent information in order to transfer the shared knowledge more efficiently and effectively. In addition, Gašić et al. (2015) presented the policy committee in order to boost the performance for policy training in a new domain. All above work extended the dialogue coverage using different directions.

Dialogue Depth Most current systems focus on knowledge-based understanding, but there are hierarchical understanding according to the dialogue complexity. For example, an intent about party scheduling may include restaurant reserving and invitation sending. Sun et al. (2016) learned the high-level intentions that span on multiple domains in order to achieve common sense understanding. Moreover, a more complex dialogue such as "*I feel sad...*" requires empathy in order to generate the suitable response. Fung et al. (2016) first attempted to leverage different modalities for emotion detection and built an emotion-aware dialogue system.

Given two branches of development, the ultimate goal is to build an open-domain dialogue system (coverage) with all levels of understanding (depth).

6 Instructors

Yun-Nung (Vivian) Chen is currently an assistant professor at the Department of Computer Science, National Taiwan University. She earned her Ph.D. degree from Carnegie Mellon University, where her research interests focus on spoken dialogue system, language understanding, natural language processing, and multi-modal speech applications. She received the Google Faculty Research Awards 2016, two Student Best Paper Awards from IEEE SLT 2010 and IEEE ASRU 2013, a Student Best Paper Nominee from Interspeech 2012, and the Distinguished Master Thesis Award from ACLCLP. Before joining National Taiwan University, she worked in the Deep Learning Technology Center at Microsoft Research Redmond. More information about her can be found at `http://vivianchen.idv.tw`.

Asli Celikyilmaz is currently a researcher at the Deep Learning Technology Center at Microsfot Research. Previously, she was a Research Scientist at Microsoft Bing from 2010 until 2016 focusing on deep learning models for scaling natural user interfaces to multiple domains. She has worked as a Postdoc Researcher at the EECS Department of the UC Berkeley from 2008 until 2010. She has worked with researchers at ICSI @ Berkeley during her postdoc research study. She has earned her Ph.D. from University of Toronto, Canada in 2008. Asli's research interests are mainly machine learning and its applications to conversational dialogue systems, mainly natural language understanding and dialogue modeling. In the past she has also focused on research areas including machine intelligence, semantic tagging of natural user utterances of human to machine conversations, text analysis, document summarization, question answering, co-reference resolution, to name a few. Currently she is focusing on reasoning, attention, memory networks as well as multi-task and transfer learning for conversational dialogue systems. She has been serving as area chair, co-organizer of numerous NLP and speech conferences, such as ACL, NAACL, Interspeech, and IEEE Spoken Language Technologies (SLT). She co-organized a NIPS workshop on Machine Learning for Spoken Language Understanding and Interactions in 2015.

Dilek Hakkani-Tür is a research scientist at Google Research. Prior to joining Google, she was a researcher at Microsoft Research (2010-2016), International Computer Science Institute (ICSI, 2006-2010) and AT&T Labs-Research (2001-2005). She received her BSc degree from Middle East Technical Univ, in 1994, and MSc and PhD degrees from Bilkent Univ., Department of Computer Engineering, in 1996 and 2000, respectively. Her research interests include natural language and speech processing, spoken dialogue systems, and machine learning for language processing. She has over 50 patents that were granted and co-authored more than 200 papers in natural language and speech processing. She is the recipient of three best paper awards for her work on active learning for dialogue systems, from IEEE Signal Processing Society, ISCA and EURASIP. She was an associate editor of IEEE Transactions on Audio, Speech and Language Processing (2005-2008), member of the IEEE Speech and Language Technical Committee (2009-2014), area editor for speech and language processing for Elsevier's Digital Signal Processing Journal and IEEE Signal Processing Letters (2011-2013), and currently serves on ISCA Advisory Council (2015-2018). She is a fellow of IEEE and ISCA.

References

Antoine Bordes and Jason Weston. 2016. Learning end-to-end goal-oriented dialog. *arXiv preprint arXiv:1605.07683* .

Ciprian Chelba, Monika Mahajan, and Alex Acero. 2003. Speech utterance classification. In *2003 IEEE International Conference on Acoustics, Speech, and Signal Processing, 2003. Proceedings.(ICASSP)*. IEEE, volume 1, pages I–280.

Yun-Nung Chen, Dilek Hakkani-T, Xiaodong He, et al. 2016a. Zero-shot learning of intent embeddings for expansion by convolutional deep structured semantic models. In *2016 IEEE International Conference on Acoustics, Speech and Signal Processing (ICASSP)*. IEEE, pages 6045–6049.

Yun-Nung Chen, Dilek Hakkani-Tur, and Gokan Tur. 2014. Deriving local relational surface forms from dependency-based entity embeddings for unsupervised spoken language understanding. In *2014 IEEE Spoken Language Technology Workshop (SLT)*. IEEE, pages 242–247.

Yun-Nung Chen, Dilek Hakkani-Tur, Gokhan Tur, Asli Celikyilmaz, Jianfeng Gao, and Li Deng. 2016b. Knowledge as a teacher: Knowledge-guided structural attention networks. *arXiv preprint arXiv:1609.03286* .

Yun-Nung Chen, Dilek Hakkani-Tür, Gokhan Tur, Jianfeng Gao, and Li Deng. 2016c. End-to-end memory networks with knowledge carryover for multi-turn spoken language understanding. In *Proceedings of the Interspeech*.

Bhuwan Dhingra, Lihong Li, Xiujun Li, Jianfeng Gao, Yun-Nung Chen, Faisal Ahmed, and Li Deng. 2016. End-to-end reinforcement learning of dialogue agents for information access. *arXiv preprint arXiv:1609.00777* .

Pascale Fung, Dario Bertero, Yan Wan, Anik Dey, Ricky Ho Yin Chan, Farhad Bin Siddique, Yang Yang, Chien-Sheng Wu, and Ruixi Lin. 2016. Towards empathetic human-robot interactions. *arXiv preprint arXiv:1605.04072* .

M Gašić, N Mrkšić, Pei-hao Su, David Vandyke, Tsung-Hsien Wen, and Steve Young. 2015. Policy committee for adaptation in multi-domain spoken dialogue systems. In *Automatic Speech Recognition and Understanding (ASRU), 2015 IEEE Workshop on*. IEEE, pages 806–812.

Patrick Haffner, Gokhan Tur, and Jerry H Wright. 2003. Optimizing svms for complex call classification. In *2003 IEEE International Conference on Acoustics, Speech, and Signal Processing, 2003. Proceedings.(ICASSP)*. IEEE, volume 1, pages I–632.

Dilek Hakkani-Tür, Gokhan Tur, Asli Celikyilmaz, Yun-Nung Chen, Jianfeng Gao, Li Deng, and Ye-Yi Wang. 2016. Multi-domain joint semantic frame parsing using bi-directional RNN-LSTM. In *Proceedings of the Interspeech*. San Francisco, CA.

Matthew Henderson, Blaise Thomson, and Steve Young. 2013. Deep neural network approach for the dialog state tracking challenge. In *Proceedings of the SIGDIAL 2013 Conference*. pages 467–471.

A. Jaech, L. Heck, and M. Ostendorf. 2016. Domain adaptation of recurrent neural networks for natural language understanding. In *Proceedings of the Interspeech*. San Francisco, CA.

Young-Bum Kim, WA Redmond, Karl Stratos, and Ruhi Sarikaya. ???? Frustratingly easy neural domain adaptation.

Xiujun Li, Yun-Nung Chen, Lihong Li, Jianfeng Gao, and Asli Celikyilmaz. 2017a. Investigation of language understanding impact for reinforcement learning based dialogue systems. *arXiv preprint arXiv:1703.07055* .

Xuijun Li, Yun-Nung Chen, Lihong Li, and Jianfeng Gao. 2017b. End-to-end task-completion neural dialogue systems. *arXiv preprint arXiv:1703.01008* .

Grégoire Mesnil, Yann Dauphin, Kaisheng Yao, Yoshua Bengio, Li Deng, Dilek Hakkani-Tur, Xiaodong He, Larry Heck, Gokhan Tur, Dong Yu, et al. 2015. Using recurrent neural networks for slot filling in spoken language understanding. *IEEE/ACM Transactions on Audio, Speech, and Language Processing* 23(3):530–539.

Nikola Mrkšić, Diarmuid Ó Séaghdha, Tsung-Hsien Wen, Blaise Thomson, and Steve Young. 2016. Neural belief tracker: Data-driven dialogue state tracking. *arXiv preprint arXiv:1606.03777* .

Alice H Oh and Alexander I Rudnicky. 2002. Stochastic natural language generation for spoken dialog systems. *Computer Speech & Language* 16(3):387–407.

Roberto Pieraccini, Evelyne Tzoukermann, Zakhar Gorelov, Jean-Luc Gauvain, Esther Levin, Chin-Hui Lee, and Jay G Wilpon. 1992. A speech understanding system based on statistical representation of semantics. In *1992 IEEE International Conference on Acoustics, Speech, and Signal Processing (ICASSP)*. IEEE, volume 1, pages 193–196.

Suman Ravuri and Andreas Stolcke. 2015. Recurrent neural network and lstm models for lexical utterance classification. In *Sixteenth Annual Conference of the International Speech Communication Association*.

Christian Raymond and Giuseppe Riccardi. 2007. Generative and discriminative algorithms for spoken language understanding. In *INTERSPEECH*. pages 1605–1608.

Alexander I Rudnicky, Eric H Thayer, Paul C Constantinides, Chris Tchou, R Shern, Kevin A Lenzo, Wei Xu, and Alice Oh. 1999. Creating natural dialogs in the carnegie mellon communicator system. In *Eurospeech*.

Ruhi Sarikaya, Geoffrey E Hinton, and Anoop Deoras. 2014. Application of deep belief networks for natural language understanding. *IEEE/ACM Transactions on Audio, Speech, and Language Processing* 22(4):778–784.

Ruhi Sarikaya, Geoffrey E Hinton, and Bhuvana Ramabhadran. 2011. Deep belief nets for natural language call-routing. In *2011 IEEE International Conference on Acoustics, Speech and Signal Processing (ICASSP)*. IEEE, pages 5680–5683.

Kai Sun, Lu Chen, Su Zhu, and Kai Yu. 2014. A generalized rule based tracker for dialogue state tracking. In *Spoken Language Technology Workshop (SLT), 2014 IEEE*. IEEE, pages 330–335.

Ming Sun, Yun-Nung Chen, and Alexander I Rudnicky. 2016. An intelligent assistant for high-level task understanding. In *Proceedings of the 21st International Conference on Intelligent User Interfaces*. ACM, pages 169–174.

Richard S Sutton and Andrew G Barto. 1998. *Reinforcement learning: An introduction*, volume 1. MIT press Cambridge.

Blaise Thomson and Steve Young. 2010. Bayesian update of dialogue state: A pomdp framework for spoken dialogue systems. *Computer Speech and Language* 24(4):562–588.

Gokhan Tur and Renato De Mori. 2011. *Spoken language understanding: Systems for extracting semantic information from speech*. John Wiley & Sons.

Gokhan Tur, Li Deng, Dilek Hakkani-Tür, and Xiaodong He. 2012. Towards deeper understanding: Deep convex networks for semantic utterance classification. In *2012 IEEE International Conference on Acoustics, Speech and Signal Processing (ICASSP)*. IEEE, pages 5045–5048.

Oriol Vinyals and Quoc Le. 2015. A neural conversational model. *arXiv preprint arXiv:1506.05869* .

Ye-Yi Wang, Li Deng, and Alex Acero. 2005. Spoken language understanding. *IEEE Signal Processing Magazine* 22(5):16–31.

Tsung-Hsien Wen, Milica Gašic, Dongho Kim, Nikola Mrkšic, Pei-Hao Su, David Vandyke, and Steve Young. 2015a. Stochastic language generation in dialogue using recurrent neural networks with convolutional sentence reranking. In *16th Annual Meeting of the Special Interest Group on Discourse and Dialogue*. page 275.

Tsung-Hsien Wen, Milica Gasic, Nikola Mrksic, Lina M Rojas-Barahona, Pei-Hao Su, Stefan Ultes, David Vandyke, and Steve Young. 2016. A network-based end-to-end trainable task-oriented dialogue system. *arXiv preprint arXiv:1604.04562*.

Tsung-Hsien Wen, Milica Gasic, Nikola Mrksic, Pei-Hao Su, David Vandyke, and Steve Young. 2015b. Semantically conditioned lstm-based natural language generation for spoken dialogue systems. *arXiv preprint arXiv:1508.01745*.

Jason D Williams and Steve Young. 2007. Partially observable markov decision processes for spoken dialog systems. *Computer Speech & Language* 21(2):393–422.

Jason D Williams and Geoffrey Zweig. 2016. End-to-end lstm-based dialog control optimized with supervised and reinforcement learning. *arXiv preprint arXiv:1606.01269*.

Puyang Xu and Ruhi Sarikaya. 2013. Convolutional neural network based triangular CRF for joint intent detection and slot filling. In *2013 IEEE Workshop on Automatic Speech Recognition and Understanding (ASRU)*. IEEE, pages 78–83.

Kaisheng Yao, Geoffrey Zweig, Mei-Yuh Hwang, Yangyang Shi, and Dong Yu. 2013. Recurrent neural networks for language understanding. In *INTERSPEECH*. pages 2524–2528.

Steve Young, Milica Gašić, Simon Keizer, François Mairesse, Jost Schatzmann, Blaise Thomson, and Kai Yu. 2010. The hidden information state model: A practical framework for pomdp-based spoken dialogue management. *Computer Speech & Language* 24(2):150–174.

Steve Young, Milica Gašić, Blaise Thomson, and Jason D Williams. 2013. POMDP-based statistical spoken dialog systems: A review. *Proceedings of the IEEE* 101(5):1160–1179.

Tiancheng Zhao and Maxine Eskenazi. 2016. Towards end-to-end learning for dialog state tracking and management using deep reinforcement learning. *arXiv preprint arXiv:1606.02560*.

Victor Zue, Stephanie Seneff, James R Glass, Joseph Polifroni, Christine Pao, Timothy J Hazen, and Lee Hetherington. 2000. JUPITER: a telephone-based conversational interface for weather information. *IEEE Transactions on speech and audio processing* 8(1):85–96.

Victor W Zue and James R Glass. 2000. Conversational interfaces: Advances and challenges. *Proceedings of the IEEE* 88(8):1166–1180.

Beyond Words: Deep Learning for Multiword Expressions and Collocations

Valia Kordoni
Humboldt-Universität zu Berlin
kordonie@anglistik.hu-berlin.de

1 Tutorial Overview

Deep learning has recently shown much promise for NLP applications. Traditionally, in most NLP approaches, documents or sentences are represented by a sparse bag-of-words representation. There is now a lot of work which goes beyond this by adopting a distributed representation of words, by constructing a so-called "neural embedding" or vector space representation of each word or document. The aim of this tutorial is to go beyond the learning of word vectors and present methods for learning vector representations for Multiword Expressions and bilingual phrase pairs, all of which are useful for various NLP applications.

This tutorial aims to provide attendees with a clear notion of the linguistic and distributional characteristics of *multiword expressions* (MWEs), their relevance for the intersection of deep learning and natural language processing, what methods and resources are available to support their use, and what more could be done in the future. Our target audience are researchers and practitioners in machine learning, parsing (syntactic and semantic) and language technology, not necessarily experts in MWEs, who are interested in tasks that involve or could benefit from considering MWEs as a pervasive phenomenon in human language and communication.

This tutorial consists of four parts. Part I starts with a thorough introduction to different types of MWEs and collocations, their linguistic dimensions (idiomaticity, syntactic and semantic fixedness, specificity, etc.), as well as their statistical characteristics (variability, recurrence, association, etc.). This part concludes with an overview of linguistic and psycholinguistic theories of MWEs to date.

For MWEs to be useful for language technology, they must be recognisable automatically. Hence, Part II surveys computational approaches to MWEs recognition, both manually-authored approaches and machine learning ones, as well as computational approaches to MWE elements combination. We will also review type and token evaluation methods for MWE identification.

Part III offers a thorough overview of how and where MWEs can contribute to the intersection of NLP and Deep Learning, particularly focusing on recent advances in the computational treatment of MWEs in the framework of Deep Learning.

Part IV of the tutorial concludes with concrete examples of where MWEs treatment can contribute to language technology applications such as machine translation, information extraction, information retrieval and parsing, as well as MWE-related multi-level annotation platforms (for instance, pipelines) and resources made available for a wide range of languages.

2 Tutorial Outline

1. PART I – General overview:
   (a) Introduction
   (b) Types and examples of MWEs and collocations
   (c) Linguistic dimensions of MWEs: idiomaticity, syntactic and semantic fixedness, specificity, etc.
   (d) Statistical dimensions of MWEs: variability, recurrence, association, etc.
   (e) Linguistic and psycholinguistic theories of MWEs

2. PART II – Computational methods (symbolic and statistical)
   (a) Recognizing the elements of MWEs
   (b) Recognising how elements are combined

Proceedings of the 55th Annual Meeting of the Association for Computational Linguistics-Tutorial Abstracts, pages 15–16
Vancouver, Canada, July 30 - August 4, 2017. ©2017 Association for Computational Linguistics
https://doi.org/10.18653/v1/P17-5005

(c) Type and token evaluation of MWE identification
(d) Robust automated natural language processing with MWEs

3. PART III – At the intersection of Deep learning and NLP
   (a) Beyond learning word vectors
   (b) Recursive Neural Networks for parsing MWEs
   (c) Learning vector representations for Multiword Expressions, grammatical relations, and bilingual phrase pairs, all of which are useful for various NLP applications

4. PART IV – Resources and applications:
   (a) MWEs in resources: corpora, lexicons and ontologies (e.g., WordNet and Genia), parsers and tools (e.g., NSP, mwetoolkit, UCS, and jMWE), and MWE website (`http://multiword.sf.net`)
   (b) Pipelines for MWE treatment: creation and annotation of resources, identification of MWEs in text, evaluation of results
   (c) MWes in Language Technology applications: Information Retrieval, Information Extraction, Machine Translation

3 Tutorial Instructor

Valia Kordoni is a research professor of computational linguistics at Humboldt University Berlin. She is a leader in EU-funded research in Machine Translation, Computational Semantics, and Machine Learning. She has organized conferences and workshops dedicated to research on MWEs, recently including the EACL 2014 *10th Workshop on Multiword Expressions (MWE 2014)* in Gothenburg, Sweden, the NAACL 2015 *11th Workshop on Multiword Expressions* in Denver, Colorado, and the ACL 2016 *12th Workshop on Multiword Expressions* in Berlin, Germany, among others. She has been the Local Chair of *ACL 2016 - The 54th Annual Meeting of the Association for Computational Linguistics* which took place at the Humboldt University Berlin in August 2016. She has taught a tutorial on *Robust Automated Natural Language Processing with Multiword Expressions and Collocations* in ACL 2013, as well as a tutorial on *Robust Semantic Analysis of Multiword Expressions with FrameNet* in EMNLP 2015, together with Miriam R. L. Petruck. She is also the author of *Multiword Expressions - From Linguistic Analysis to Language Technology Applications* (to appear, Springer).

Tutorial: Making Better Use of the Crowd

Jennifer Wortman Vaughan
Microsoft Research
jenn@microsoft.com

1 Overview

Over the last decade, crowdsourcing has been used to harness the power of human computation to solve tasks that are notoriously difficult to solve with computers alone, such as determining whether or not an image contains a tree, rating the relevance of a website, or verifying the phone number of a business.

The natural language processing and machine learning communities were early to embrace crowdsourcing as a tool for quickly and inexpensively obtaining annotated data to train systems. Once this data is collected, it can be handed off to algorithms that learn to perform basic tasks such as translation or parsing.

Many times this handoff is where interaction with the crowd ends. The crowd provides the data, but the ultimate goal is to eventually take humans out of the loop. Are there better ways to make use of the crowd?

In this tutorial, I will begin with a showcase of innovative uses of crowdsourcing that go beyond data collection and annotation. I will discuss direct applications to natural language processing and machine learning, hybrid intelligence or "human in the loop" AI systems, and large scale studies of human behavior in online systems.

I will then dive into recent research aimed at understanding who crowdworkers are, how they behave, and what this can teach us about best practices for interacting with the crowd.

I will debunk the common myth that crowdsourcing platforms are riddled with bad actors out to scam requesters. In particular, I will describe the results of a research study that showed that crowdworkers on the whole are basically honest, and describe what requestors can do to encourage this honest behavior.

I will talk about experiments that have explored how to boost the quality and quantity of crowdwork by appealing to both well-designed monetary incentives (such as performance-based payments) and intrinsic sources of motivation (such as curiosity or a sense of doing meaningful work).

I will then discuss recent research—both qualitative and quantitative—that has opened up the black box of crowdsourcing to uncover that crowdworkers are not independent contractors, but rather a network of workers with a rich communication structure.

Taken as a whole, this research has a lot to teach us about how to most effectively interact with the crowd. Throughout the tutorial, I will discuss best practices for engaging with crowdworkers that are rarely mentioned in the literature but make a huge difference in whether or not your research studies succeed. (A few hints: Be respectful. Be responsive. Be clear.)

All material associated with the tutorial will be available at: `http://www.jennwv.com/projects/crowdtutorial.html`

2 Tutorial Outline

Part 1: The Potential of Crowdsourcing

- Direct applications to NLP and machine learning
- Hybrid intelligence systems
- Large-scale studies of human behavior online

Part 2: The Crowd is Made of People

- Crowdworker demographics
- Honesty of crowdworkers
- Monetary incentives
- Intrinsic motivation
- The network within the crowd
- Discussion and additional best practices

Proceedings of the 55th Annual Meeting of the Association for Computational Linguistics-Tutorial Abstracts, pages 17–18
Vancouver, Canada, July 30 - August 4, 2017.
https://doi.org/10.18653/v1/P17-5006

3 Instructor's Bio

Jenn Wortman Vaughan is a Senior Researcher at Microsoft Research, New York City, where she studies algorithmic economics, machine learning, and social computing, with a heavy focus on prediction markets and other forms of crowdsourcing. She is interested in developing general methods that allow us to reason formally about the performance of algorithms with human components in the same way that traditional computer science techniques allow us to formally reason about algorithms that run on machines alone. Jenn came to Microsoft in 2012 from UCLA, where she was an assistant professor in the computer science department. She completed her Ph.D. at the University of Pennsylvania in 2009, and subsequently spent a year as a Computing Innovation Fellow at Harvard. She is the recipient of Penn's 2009 Rubinoff dissertation award for innovative applications of computer technology, a National Science Foundation CAREER award, a Presidential Early Career Award for Scientists and Engineers (PECASE), and a handful of best paper or best student paper awards. In her "spare" time, Jenn is involved in a variety of efforts to provide support for women in computer science; most notably, she co-founded the Annual Workshop for Women in Machine Learning, which has been held each year since 2006.

References and Other Material

Please see the tutorial website: `http://www.jennwv.com/projects/crowdtutorial.html`

Author Index

Association for Computational Linguistics
209 N. Eighth Street
Stroudsburg, Pennsylvania 18360

ISBN 978-1-5108-4571-8

9 781510 845718

CURRAN ASSOCIATES INC.
proceedings
.com